The S

The Sayings series

Jane Austen
Charlotte Brontë
Lord Byron
Lewis Carroll
Winston Churchill
Charles Dickens
Benjamin Disraeli
F. Scott Fitzgerald
Benjamin Franklin
Goethe
Thomas Hardy
Henrik Ibsen
Dr Johnson
James Joyce
John Keats
Rudyard Kipling
D.H. Lawrence
Somerset Maugham
Friedrich Nietzsche
George Orwell
Dorothy Parker
Samuel Pepys
Ezra Pound
Sir Walter Scott
William Shakespeare
George Bernard Shaw
Sydney Smith
R.L. Stevenson
Jonathan Swift
Leo Tolstoy
Anthony Trollope
Mark Twain
Evelyn Waugh
Oscar Wilde
Virginia Woolf
W.B. Yeats
The Bible
The Buddha
Jesus
Moses
Muhammad

The Sayings of

GOETHE

edited by
D.J. Enright

DUCKWORTH

First published in 1996 by
Gerald Duckworth & Co. Ltd.
The Old Piano Factory
48 Hoxton Square, London N1 6PB
Tel: 0171 729 5986
Fax: 0171 729 0015

Introduction, translations and editorial arrangement
© 1996 by D.J. Enright

All rights reserved. No part of this publication
may be reproduced, stored in a retrieval system, or
transmitted, in any form or by any means, electronic,
mechanical, photocopying, recording or otherwise,
without the prior permission of the publisher.

A catalogue record for this book is available
from the British Library

ISBN 0 7156 2745 7

Typeset by Ray Davies
Printed and bound in Great Britain by
Booksprint

Contents

7 Introduction
13 Society
18 Men & Women
21 Youth & Age
24 The Germans
26 The English & Other Foreigners
30 The Individual & the World
33 The Deed
36 Authors & Audiences
41 The Arts & Translation
44 Religion
48 Nature & Science
51 War & Revolution
53 Freedom, Law & Order
56 Truths & Errors
60 The Man Himself

In memoriam
COLIN HAYCRAFT
1929-1994

Introduction

Goethe lived from 1749 to 1832. In 1780 he wrote to Frau von Stein, his platonic mistress and in some respects Egeria, of the great gift of the gods: that the rapidity and variety of his thoughts enabled him to split a single day into a million parts, making an eternity in miniature. He lived at that time, and for a long time, faithfully performing his diverse duties as a privy councillor, in the small provincial state of Saxe-Weimar, a serviceable microcosm for one whose intellectual province was to be the world. His scientific writings alone occupy thirteen volumes of the Weimar edition: on colour, morphology, meteorology, mineralogy, plant and animal life, and his discovery of the intermaxillary (upper-jaw) bone in man. His curiosity was boundless and unflagging, and his perception often acute in the extreme. In 1827 he came close to predicting the Panama Canal, and declared that he would like to see Britain 'in possession of a canal through the Isthmus of Suez'.

What characterises Goethe's scientific thinking is his belief in the continuity of nature, the merging of life into life, as witness the intermaxillary bone, previously thought to be absent from man and thus separating him from the animals. The drive towards unity by way of process ('nothing stands still') is implicit in all his work, while in his literary writings ample room is found for multiplicity, contradiction and strife. Thomas Mann defined his overriding greatness as the fruit of a happy and probably unique union of 'the daemonic and the urbane'; the notion of Goethe as the cool and collected (and complacent) sage, all ego and no id, is remote from the reality. His epigrams and maxims vary strikingly in theme and tone, from the stern, authoritarian and assured to the mischievous, coarse or pugnacious, the questioning and the anguished. 'When Goethe becomes an Apollo, he becomes a plaster cast': there is a grain of truth in D.H. Lawrence's charge. In later life he was so commonly approached as an Olympian, 'Europe's sagest head, Physician of the Iron Age' (Matthew Arnold), that he could hardly avoid behaving like one at times, especially no doubt when irked by such soliciting; but it would be a very tendentious reading that could represent him, even to our modernly iconoclastic gaze, as habitually a plaster cast. 'If one employs this word "sage" with all the care and scruple it deserves,' T.S. Eliot has said, 'then one has in mind one of the rarest achievements of the human spirit'; Goethe was certainly of his age, yet also, by virtue of being above it, 'about as unrepresentative of his age as a man of genius can be'.

Writing to Charlotte von Stein on 1 May 1780, Goethe enclosed a poem and a drawing of a pigsty, with the message, 'I am sending you the highest and the lowest ... Love links all things.' Mephistopheles himself has a place in the grand design: men are all too apt to sink into inertia, says the Lord in the Prologue to *Faust*, and Mephistopheles, devilishly creative, spurs them into activity. If the unity of Goethe's thinking is far from apparent, it is precisely because of its universality, because so many disparate and often unexpected phenomena are subsumed in that whole. His animus against revolution, but also against the misrule that provokes it, is mirrored amusingly in Henry Crabb Robinson's account of a meeting in 1804, when Goethe initially surprised him by defending the comic scenes in Otway's *Venice Preserv'd*, generally omitted in English productions of the play. Though poor, he said, the scenes were essential in that they showed how utterly unfit for government the Senate had become and hence went some way to justifying the conspiracy.

Goethe once informed a visitor that he was an atheist in natural science and philosophy, a pagan in art, and a Christian by sentiment. By sentiment, we note, rather than by intellectual conviction. He respected devout individuals, and conducted himself tactfully towards them, but had little respect for the professional representatives of religion. That all things were progressively created by the same hand, as it were, is central to his thought. If some people came to consider him godlike, that was their affair. One might at least feel he was privy to the Creator, particularly if the latter was to be accorded a measure of irony. 'May God be patient with me as heretofore': the tone of the remark is ambiguous, but it includes an element of sturdy egalitarianism and independence. Perhaps he was sufficiently akin to his Creator – if he strayed, at all events he strove untiringly – to be reasonably sure that God, whatever form He might take, wouldn't be too discontented with him. His own creativity was continuous and organic. It is something of a commonplace that Goethe's longer works hardly ever achieve unmistakable success as a whole – like individual lives, they come to a halt rather than to completion: there was always more waiting to be said – and that what he excels in as a finished and finishing artist are the elegies, ballads and lyrics (which generally bear out his reservations concerning translatability, though David Luke's *Roman Elegies* are an exception), to which for present purposes we may add his letters, autobiographical writings, epigrams and scattered gnomic sayings, and (with due caution) his recorded conversations.

No single life, no intellectual life and character, has been more minutely chronicled and analysed than Goethe's. Over decades he was the object of close attention by a host of witnesses, for the most part intelligent, knowledgeable, and considerable writers, among them Friedrich von Müller, Chancellor of Saxe-Weimar and a man of the world who brought out Goethe's sardonic side. The most famous of them, though not the most distinguished socially or intellectually, was Johann Peter Eckermann, whose *Conversations* appeared in two volumes in 1836 with a supplement in 1848. Born in 1792, of humble parentage, Eckermann made his way to Weimar in 1823 and worked devotedly as Goethe's unofficial secretary during the remaining nine years of the poet's life. To us the *Conversations* may – at times must – smack of idealising, and of idolising, but Nietzsche called it 'the best German book ever written'. It is surely one of the meatiest.

Goethe told Müller that Eckermann knew best how to extract literary work from him, 'by the intelligent interest he takes in what I have already done and already begun'. Eckermann possessed a gift comparable to James Boswell's for eliciting responses and sustaining and steering the discourse. In March 1825 Goethe, who in earlier years had managed the Weimar theatre, related how he had been passionately attracted to a number of the actresses, rich in physical and mental charms, and it often happened that he was met halfway. He pulled himself together and said, 'No further!' For in this connection he was not a private person, but the director of an institution whose prosperity counted for more than any momentary gratification. 'Had I involved myself in some love affair, I would have become like a compass that cannot point aright when influenced by a magnet lying alongside it.' This 'confession' touched Eckermann deeply, causing him, he says, to love and revere his master all the more. We might think of the moment in Boswell's *Life of Johnson* when he records his subject's remark to David Garrick about the silk stockings and white bosoms of the Drury Lane actresses exciting his 'amorous propensities'. A closer parallel is between the story of Johnson setting about Bishop Berkeley's theory of the unreality of material objects by kicking a large stone – 'I refute it *thus*' – and Goethe's expostulation to Schopenhauer: 'Light exists only in so far as you see it? No! You wouldn't exist if the light did not see you.' (The great realist, indeed: his poems, he insisted, sprang from actual occasions, and all his works were 'fragments of a great confession'.) Just as Eckermann was a more solemn and deliberate chronicler than Boswell, so Goethe was more conscious than Johnson of addressing himself to posterity.

Obviously it is unsafe to cite as 'the sayings' of any author passages culled from fiction or plays or even poetry. But much less so than usual in the case of Goethe, who customarily involved himself in the characters or the circumstances he portrayed. (Nothing, one would say, could be further from the man than his Werther, yet he had been uncomfortably close to Werther, and Wilhelm Meister is confessedly both 'a poor specimen' and the author himself; if Goethe was a representative man, he contrived to represent many kinds of men, and some kinds of women.) In extracting 'sayings' from two novels, at least, we have express authority. In *Wilhelm Meister's Travels*, the sections called 'From Makarie's Archive' and 'Reflections in the Mind of the Wanderers' both consist of unpublished material from Goethe's archives, selected by Eckermann to 'fill the gaps' in the expanded version of the novel published in 1829 as part of the collected works in forty volumes. And of the journal kept by Ottilie in *Elective Affinities* it is observed by the narrator that most of the aphorisms couldn't have arisen in her own youthful mind and very probably she copied them from some book.

However malicious the intent of Mephistopheles' words, 'Grey, dear friend, is all theory,/And green the golden tree of life', when addressed to the freshman who is lamenting the absence from the campus of trees and greenery, we recognise the sentiment as distinctly one of Goethe's own. Similarly, when in the Second Part of *Faust* Mephistopheles comments on the battle of Pharsalus, 'They're fighting, so it's said, for liberty;/It's slaves fight slaves, on closer scrutiny', while he is demonstrating his standard cynicism regarding human endeavour, he is also voicing Goethe's view of revolution, as conveyed in the epigram: 'The masses were tyrants to the masses.' Goethe agreed with a critic who noted that the scorn and bitter irony of Mephistopheles were a part of himself; and a travelling companion observed that an angel looked out of one of his eyes and a devil out of the other.

Goethe was what today we would term 'a good European', and more, a citizen of the world, as his high regard for translation suggests. (In 1827 he told Eckermann that he had just been reading something in French which made him think, 'This man speaks rather cleverly, one wouldn't have expressed it otherwise.' Looking at the passage more closely, he recognised it as a translation from his own writings.) The notion of him as a narrow-minded stuffed shirt will scarcely survive exposure to the libertine goings-on in the Wilhelm Meister novels, the unorthodox views on marriage and passion aired in *Elective Affinities*, or his surpassing admiration for

Byron (who should have lived to dramatise the Old Testament: 'What a subject under his hands would the Tower of Babel have been!' he told Robinson in 1829), let alone the erotic poems and epigrams. His aesthetic liberality is manifest in a disquisition on *Macbeth* recorded by Eckermann (18 April 1827). It doesn't trouble Shakespeare, he said, that Macduff's words, 'He has no children!', contradict those of Lady Macbeth. What counts is the force of the speech, and just as Macduff needs to give the utmost emphasis to what he is saying, so to the same end Lady Macbeth must say, 'I have given suck ...' We shouldn't dwell too precisely and punctiliously on a painter's brushwork or the niceties of poetic composition, but 'when a work of art has been created in a bold and free spirit, we should rather aim to apprehend and enjoy it in a similar spirit'. Akin is his insistence that introspection and self-examination – sins against the daemon – deter us from activity and fulfilment, expressed pungently in a remark to Eckermann: 'I don't know myself, and God forbid that I should.'

Faced with individual persons and specific situations, Goethe often seems to be adumbrating a general law without defining it, and certainly without imposing it. The impression – by no means irreconcilable with his debunking of 'originality' – is that his insights into human nature, as into art and science, are not borrowed but earned in person. That he reiterated the need for self-mastery was because there was much in him to control. And if it is the aura of *health* surrounding him that puts us off, we should remember that it wasn't easily won, and we should think of where sickness has got us.

Sources and abbreviations

I have chiefly used the Artemis Verlag 'Gedenkausgabe' of Goethe's works (1948 onwards), with some recourse to the Hamburg edition (1948 onwards) and the Weimar ('Sophien') edition (143 volumes, 1887-1920).

Main works from which passages are drawn:

Art and Antiquity (*Über Kunst und Altertum*), series of miscellaneous volumes edited by Goethe, 1816-32: referred to as *AA*.

Conversations with Goethe (*Gespräche mit Goethe in den letzten Jahren seines Lebens*), Johann Peter Eckermann, 1836, 1848: *E*.

Elective Affinities (*Die Wahlverwandtschaften*), 1809: *EA*; 'Ottilie's Journal': *EA:OJ*.

Epigrams (miscellaneous), 1810 onwards: *ME*.

Faust Part One (*Faust, der Tragödie erster Teil*), 1808: *F1*.

Faust Part Two (*Faust, der Tragödie zweiter Teil*), 1832: *F2*.

Italian Journey (*Die Italienische Reise*), published 1816-17, but entries dated according to events during 1786-8: *IJ*.

Poetry and Truth (*Dichtung und Wahrheit*), in four parts, 1811, 1812, 1814, 1833: *PAT*.

Sayings in Prose (*Sprüche in Prosa*; also known as *Maximen und Reflexionen*), published posthumously: *SIP*.

Venetian Epigrams (*Venezianische Epigramme*), written 1790: *VE*.

Wilhelm Meister's Apprenticeship (*Wilhelm Meisters Lehrjahre*), 1795-6: *WMA*.

Wilhelm Meister's Travels (*Wilhelm Meisters Wanderjahre*), enlarged version, 1829: *WMT*; 'From Makarie's Archive' ('Aus Makariens Archiv'): *WMT:MA*; 'Reflections in the Mind of the Wanderers' ('Betrachtungen im Sinne der Wanderer'): *WMT:RMW*.

In fictional works, when passages cited are spoken by a character as distinct from the narrator, the character's name is given. In extracts from conversations, the informant is named; extracts from Goethe's letters are marked 'Letter to …'.

I am indebted to Helmut Winter for help on some tricky points of meaning.

Society

Had it been God's intention that men should live and act in the way of truth, he would have had to make different arrangements.
SIP

You can force anything on society, so long as it has no consequences.
EA:OJ

> It happened, during some grand party,
> A quiet scholar left the others early.
> When asked what he had thought of them,
> 'Were they books,' he said, 'I wouldn't read 'em.'
>
> 'Society', *ME*

We wouldn't say much in company if we realised how often we misunderstand what the others say.
EA:OJ

Perhaps misunderstandings and inertia cause more mischief in the world than cunning and malice. At all events, the latter are less common.
The Sorrows of Young Werther, 1774; Werther

Everyone has something in his nature which, if openly expressed, would inevitably give offence.
AA, 1821

One cannot live for everybody, least of all for those with whom one wouldn't want to live.
AA, 1823

In no way do people reveal their characters more clearly than through what they find ridiculous.
EA:OJ

He who feels no love must learn to flatter, or else he won't get by.
AA, 1823

Through what we call deportment and good manners we attain that which otherwise is to be attained only by force, if that.
EA:OJ

There is a politeness of the heart; it is related to love. From it springs the most agreeable politeness of outward behaviour.
Ibid.

It wouldn't be a bad idea to insert in future books of etiquette, after the chapters on how to behave when in company, a detailed chapter on how to conduct ourselves in art collections and museums.

EA; Ottilie

People take note only of those through whom they have suffered. To go around unremarked in the world one merely has to have hurt no one. *SIP*

We are never deceived, we deceive ourselves.

WMT:MA

We are willing to acknowledge our shortcomings, we are willing to be punished for them, we patiently suffer much on their account, but we grow impatient if we are required to renounce them.

EA:OJ

We cannot rid ourselves of what belongs to us, even if we throw it away.

WMT:MA

When a man thinks about his physical or moral state, he usually finds himself sick.

AA, 1821

Happily a human being can take in misfortune only up to a certain degree; what goes beyond this either destroys him or leaves him indifferent.

EA

We never realise how anthropomorphic we are.

AA, 1823

Pederasty being as old as mankind, we can say that it is in nature, even though it is against nature.

Friedrich von Müller, 7 April 1830

We must cultivate our qualities, not our idiosyncrasies.

SIP

A great mistake: to fancy oneself to be more than one is, and to value oneself at less than one is worth.

WMT:RMW

Society

We see that for the most part emigrants carry their faults and foolish habits along with them, and we wonder at it. But as the English traveller in whatever quarter of the globe never leaves his tea-kettle behind, so the mass of mankind are everywhere accompanied by haughty demands, vanity, intemperance, impatience, obstinacy, distorted judgement, and the desire to get the better of their fellow men by guile.

Entertainments of German Emigrants, 1795

Nothing is more odious than the majority; for it consists of a few energetic pacemakers, of rogues who accommodate themselves, of weaklings who join in, and of the masses who trot behind without knowing in the slightest what they want.

WMT:RMW

As in Rome, aside from the Romans, there is a race of statues, so apart from this real world there is a world of illusion, almost more potent, in which most people live.

AA, 1826

We love our friends, we esteem them, we are even ready on occasion to render them a substantial service at some cost to ourselves. But when it comes to some fleeting fancy, some playful conceit, some whim of theirs, we are – how shall I say? – too lazy, too indifferent, too dull, too genteel, and we don't realise that it is the satisfaction of just these strange-seeming cravings which affords the greatest relish.

Letter to Marianne von Eybenberg, 4 April 1803

I am already getting on better with other people. We should remember always to weigh them in the grocer's scales and never in the goldsmith's balance, as alas friends in hypochondriac or over-rigorous spirit are too wont to do with one another.

IJ, 17 March 1787

It isn't enough that we can risk our life to serve a friend; if need be, we should also sacrifice our convictions for him.

WMA; Wilhelm

Nobody should cast a stone at his neighbour; and nobody should compose long speeches with a view to shaming people, unless he utters them in front of a looking-glass.

WMA; Jarno

Advice is a peculiar business. When you have seen how in the world the most judicious enterprises miscarry and the most absurd often come to fruition, you draw back from giving advice to anybody. A person should give advice only in matters where he will cooperate. If anybody asks me for advice, I say I am ready to give it, but only on condition that he promises me not to act on it.

E, 13 February 1831

I too am convinced that humanity will win in the end; I only fear that at the same time the world will turn into a vast hospital and each of us become his neighbour's attentive nurse.

Letter to Charlotte von Stein, 8 June 1787

A genuine universal tolerance is most surely attained if we let rest the peculiarities of individual men and races and hold fast to the conviction that what has true merit is distinguished by its belonging to all mankind.

Letter to Thomas Carlyle, 20 July 1827

We know that we exist only when we find ourselves again in others.

Letter to Countess Auguste Stolberg, 13 February 1775

For the vast superiority of another there is no remedy but love.

EA:OJ

What does a human life in abstract amount to? In the presence of the simple particulars of a significant life, all pragmatic biographical sketches must creep away into a hole.

Letter to Johann Heinrich Meyer, 8 February 1796

It requires talent even to produce what isn't satisfying. And in my view errors merge into something good, as is also the case when we look closely at individuals; we always find cause to praise and blame them, and yet in the end we have to love them.

Letter to Karl Friedrich von Reinhard, 28 August 1807

Man wouldn't be the noblest creature on the earth if he weren't too noble for it.

AA, 1821

How could man live if he did not give absolution every evening to himself and others?

Müller, 6 December 1825

Let mankind last as long as it may, it will never lack obstacles to keep it busy, and never be short of necessity in all sorts of forms to develop its powers. Men will become more clever and more acute; but not better, happier, or more vigorous, or at any rate only in epochs. I foresee the time when God will have no more joy in them, and will once again smash up everything for a rejuvenated creation.

E, 23 October 1828

Men & Women

There is no doubt that in all civilised nations women on the whole must gain the ascendancy, for by reciprocal influence the man must become more feminine, and loses thereby since his merit lies not in moderate but in mastered strength. On the other hand, when the woman takes something from the man, it is to her advantage, for if she can raise her other qualities through energy, a being emerges who could not be more complete.
>   'The Good Women', 1800; Armidoro, a young gentleman

> Where morality reigns, there women reign.
> Where impudence rules, women are as nothing.
>   *Torquato Tasso*, 1790; the Princess

Understanding and reason are formal powers, the heart furnishes the content, the matter. If we can regard men as understanding and reason, then they are form; women, as heart, are matter.
>   Friedrich Wilhelm Riemer, 15 January 1810

Men and women need a different Saviour.   *PAT*, 1814

Women are silver dishes into which we put golden apples.
>   *E*, 22 October 1828

In each sex there is a cruelty towards the other, which perhaps stirs in every individual at times without being able to vent itself directly. In men it is the cruelty of lust, in women the cruelty of ingratitude, obtuse tormenting, etc.
>   Riemer, 7 July 1811

What does it matter if a few couples beat each other and make life a misery, provided the general idea of the sanctity of marriage is maintained? After all, these individuals would have other troubles to bear if they were rid of their present ones.   Müller, 7 April 1830

The reasons of a girl who draws back always seem valid, those of a man never.
>   *PAT*, 1814; on breaking with Friederike Brion in 1771

The arrows of Eros work in diverse ways: some of them
  scratch,
    And from the creeping poison year by year the heart
      sickens.
But with powerfully feathered shafts and tips freshly
  sharpened,
    Others pierce through to the quick, swiftly kindling the
      blood.

Roman Elegies, 1788-90

I know you, Eros, as well as anyone. You arrive
  With your torch, and it shines before us in the dark,
But soon you lead us down tortuous paths. And when
  We really need that torch, the traitor goes out.

VE

Love is so strong a spice that even stale or nauseating broths are made palatable by it.

WMA

To woo on behalf of another is a ticklish matter.

Hermann and Dorothea, 1797; the parson

The God who made both lads and lasses
Likewise knew that noblest of professions –
How to bring about occasions.

F1; Mephistopheles

As if love had anything to do with the intellect! The things we love in a young woman are quite other than that. We love her beauty, youth, playfulness, trustfulness, her character, faults, caprices, and God knows what else and inexpressible besides. The intellect may serve to bind us when we already love, but it isn't what arouses a passion in us.

E, 2 January 1824

An epigram's too short to convey anything heartfelt?
  Yet, darling, isn't a heartfelt kiss even shorter?

Four Seasons, c. 1797

So rejoice, you who are living, in the place that's warmed by
  love,
    Before dread Lethe coldly splashes your fleeing foot.

Roman Elegies, 1788-90

Whatever as truth or fable
A thousand books provide,
All is but a tower of Babel
Except what love has unified.

Tame Xenia, 1820-7

The Eternal Womanly
Draws us on high.

F2; Chorus Mysticus: closing lines

Youth & Age

If we want to see through the eyes of others in the manner of Swedenborg's spirits, it's best to choose the eyes of children.
Letter to his mother, 3 October 1785

The major maxim of pedagogy: not to disturb children, or the un- and half-educated, in their reverence for higher things.
Diaries, 24 April 1831

We should deal with children as God does with us, making us happiest under the influence of kindly delusions.
The Sorrows of Young Werther, 1774; Werther

We cannot fashion our children after our own thinking;
Just as God gave them, so must we take them and love them.
Hermann and Dorothea, 1797; the mother

If children grew up in accordance with early indications, we should have nothing but geniuses.
PAT, 1811

Everyone believes in his youth that the world really began with him and that everything really exists for his sake alone.
E, 6 December 1829

The most foolish of errors is for clever young people to think they lose their originality by accepting some truth which has already been accepted by others.
AA, 1824

Youth is drunkenness without wine.
The West-Eastern Divan, 1819

Young people are nature's new aperçus.
SIP

If youth is a fault, it is one we put aside soon enough.

Ibid.

The man who expects so much in his youth doesn't deceive himself. But as he then found the anticipation of things in his heart, so now he must seek the fulfilment in his heart, not outside himself.

Ibid.

People always suppose we must grow old to become wise; but in reality, as the years advance, it is hard to stay as wise as we were. True, in the various stages of his life a man becomes a different being; but he cannot claim he is a better one, and in certain matters he is as likely to be right in his twentieth year as in his sixtieth.

E, 17 February 1831

> Age doesn't make us childish, as they say,
> It only shows that we're true children still.
>
> *F1, Prelude on the Stage; the Clown*

One merely has to grow old to become more lenient; I see no error made which I too might not have committed.

AA, 1824

If in old age intelligent and thoughtful persons set little store by knowledge, it is only because they have asked too much of it and of themselves.

AA, 1821

It doesn't become the ageing man to pursue fashion either in ways of thinking or in ways of dressing. But he should know where he stands and what the others are driving at.

SIP

Growing older in itself means entering on a new business; all the circumstances change, and one must either give up activity altogether or assume the new role with awareness and intention.

AA, 1825

The old lose one of the prime rights of man: they will no longer be judged by their own kind.

AA, 1826

Youth & Age

A burnt child fears the fire; an old man who has often been scorched is afraid of warming himself.

SIP

It is with the years as with the Sibylline books: the more they are consumed, the more precious they become.

Ibid.

It wouldn't be worth the trouble of being seventy years old if all the wisdom of the world were folly before God.

WMT:MA

The Germans

It is in the nature of the Germans that they weigh heavily on everything, that everything weighs heavily on them.
WMA; Aurelia

Germany can't escape from itself, even if it runs away to Rome; it will always be accompanied by its platitudes like the Englishman by his tea-kettle.
Letter to Friedrich Schiller, 30 December 1795

What must the English and the French think of the language of our philosophers, when we Germans don't understand them ourselves!
E, 28 March 1827

The Germans are strange people! By their deep thoughts and ideas, which they look for everywhere and read into everything, they make life more burdensome than needs be.
E, 6 May 1827

Recently, when the snow had settled and my neighbour's children wanted to try out their little sledges on the street, a policeman promptly turned up, and I saw the poor little things scurry off as fast as they could. Now that the spring sunshine entices them out of doors and they would like to play with one another in front of their houses, I can see they are perpetually uneasy, as if fearing the arrival of some police potentate. No lad may crack a whip or sing or shout, but the police are at once on hand to forbid it. The result is to tame youth prematurely and drive out all nature, all originality and all wildness, so that in the end nothing is left but the philistine.
E, 12 March 1828; a comparison with the 'far freer development' enjoyed by English children

A German writer, a German martyr!
E, 14 March 1830

To be polite in German is to lie.
F2; the Bachelor of Arts

> A true-born German can't abide the Frenchies,
> Their wines however he still relishes.
>
> *F1*, Auerbach's Tavern; Brander

Germany herself stands so high in every field that we can scarcely take it all in, and now we must be Greeks and Latins, and Englishmen and Frenchmen to boot. On top of which, some people are crazy enough to point to the East as well, which is enough to befuddle any young fellow.

E, 15 February 1824

Germany is nothing, but every individual German is much, and yet they fancy the reverse of this to be true. Like the Jews, the Germans must be transplanted and scattered all over the world, in order to develop their great gifts fully and for the benefit of all nations.

Müller, 14 December 1808

The English & Other Foreigners

The English are perhaps better suited than others to impress foreigners. Their personal calm, self-assurance, activeness, and prosperity present a practically unattainable model of what all people would wish for themselves.
Theory of Colour, 1810

We learn of everything that is going on in the world, and how and why. Englishmen tell us about it with the greatest sang-froid, because they know that the world belongs to them.
Letter to Meyer, 29 October 1817

Here in Weimar we see only a few Englishmen, and probably by no means the best; but what fine handsome people they are! And though they are as young as seventeen when they arrive, they feel in no way strange or embarrassed in this foreign land. On the contrary, their manner in society is as full of confidence and ease as if they were masters everywhere and the whole world belonged to them. This is what pleases our women, and why they create such havoc in the hearts of our young ladies.
E, 12 March 1828

This is the advantage one has with the English, that they know how to distinguish at once between the useful and the useless.
Letter to Thomas Johann Seebeck, 30 December 1819

The Englishman is the master in at once using what is discovered until it leads on to a new discovery and fresh achievements. We now ask why they are everywhere ahead of us.
WMT:RMW

As a rule the English write well, being born orators and practical men, and tending towards the real.
E, 14 April 1824

Tea always acts as a poison on me. And yet where would women be without it? Making tea is a kind of function, an imaginary occupation, especially in England. And there they sit around, so comfortable and pale and beautiful and tall, and there we must just leave them to sit.
Müller, 1 May 1826

The English & Other Foreigners

People reproach the English with carrying their tea-kettles wherever they go, even lugging them up Mount Etna. But doesn't every nation have its tea-kettle in which, even while travelling abroad, it steeps its dried bundle of herbs brought from home?

Winckelmann and his Century, 1805

Truly speaking, all Englishmen are, as such, without reflection; distractions and party spirit prevent them from developing themselves in peace. But they are great as practical men.

E, 24 February 1825

The British parliament consists of strong opposing powers which paralyse one another, and where the great insight of an individual has difficulty in working its way through.

E, 9 July 1827

His book will in no sense be a document for the history of France, but it will be one for the history of England.

Frédéric Soret, 22 January 1830; of Walter Scott's *Life of Napoleon*.

Nowhere are there so many hypocrites and pharisees as in England; it may have been different in Shakespeare's time, however.

Friedrich Förster, May 1829

It is astonishing to observe how large a portion of the life of a rich Englishman of rank is passed in abductions and duels. Lord Byron himself says that his father carried off three ladies. And let any man be a sensible son after that.

E, 24 February 1825

People think to name me in so many ways –
Are there Britons here? Travel's their specialty ...
They would bear witness: in their mystery plays
I used to appear as 'Old Iniquity'.

F2, Classical Walpurgis Night; Mephistopheles

It's a pleasure to see how the earlier pedantry of the Scots has changed into seriousness and depth.

E, 11 October 1828; of an article on himself by Carlyle

We can't be really clear about the state of Ireland since the subject is too involved. But so much we can see: that she suffers from evils which cannot be cured by any means, including emancipation. If it has hitherto been a misfortune for her to endure her evils alone, it is now a misfortune that England is drawn into them too. We see what a hard time the two million Protestants in Ireland have had thus far against the preponderance of five million Catholics. The Catholics don't get along among themselves, but they always unite against a Protestant.

E, 7 April 1829

> Need teaches prayer, they say; if you want to learn, then go
> To Italy! The stranger is bound to meet need.
>
> *VE*

The Israelite people has never amounted to much, as it was told a thousand times reproachfully by its rulers, judges, teachers and prophets. It possesses few virtues, and most of the faults of other peoples. However, in its self-reliance, firmness, courage, and – when all this no longer avails – doggedness, it has no equal.

WMT; the Eldest

The Chinese think, act, and feel almost as we do, and we very soon find we resemble them, except that everything goes on more clearly, purely and morally with them. With them everything is judicious, citizen-like, without strong passion or poetic sweep. There are countless legends, all turning on what is moral and seemly. It is by this strict moderation in all things that the Chinese Empire has maintained itself for thousands of years and will continue to survive.

E, 31 January 1827; Goethe had just been reading a Chinese novel

> Use the present to happy effect!
> And your children, when they grow into poets,
> May a benevolent fate protect
> From stories of knights and robbers and spirits.
>
> 'America, you are better off/Than our old continent', 1827

With intercourse now so close among the French, English and Germans, it is very pleasing to see that we shall be able to correct one another. This is the great benefit of a world-literature, which will show itself more and more.

E, 15 July 1827

The history of knowledge is a great fugue in which the voices of the nations gradually make their appearance.

WMT:RMW

The Individual & the World

Mankind? That is an abstraction. It has always been individual men and women alone who existed, and it will always be so.
Heinrich Luden, 19 August 1806

To say that each man should sacrifice himself to the good of all seems to me a false principle. Each man should sacrifice himself to his own conviction.
Soret, 20 October 1830; adding that the general good might ensue

Genuine conviction springs from the heart. As the true seat of conscience, the heart is a far more reliable judge of what is permissible than the understanding. The latter, for all its discernment and decisiveness, is likely to miss the real point.
Letter to Carlyle, 14 March 1828

A talent is formed in tranquillity,
Character in the current of the world.
Torquato Tasso, 1790; Leonora Sanvitale

The greatest humans are always linked to their age by some weakness. *EA:OJ*

Let no man think that people have awaited him as the messiah!
SIP

For every bird there is a bait, and every man is led and misled in his own way. *PAT*, 1811

Two souls alas! are living in my breast,
The one desires to break free from the other.
F1; Faust

The man who becomes a god cannot go on living, nor ought he, for his own sake and that of others.
Letter to Charlotte von Stein, 19 December 1781;
on the death of Captain Cook

Love of self makes us imagine both our virtues and our faults more important than they are.
WMA

The Individual & the World

He who doesn't fancy himself too much is more than he fancies.
AA, 1821

When others in their agony fall silent
A god empowered me to tell my pain.
Torquato Tasso, 1790; Tasso

Mastery is often taken for egoism. *AA*, 1826

But how would the deity continually find opportunity to work wonders, if he didn't at times try his hand on extraordinary individuals, at whom we gaze astonished, unable to understand where they come from?
E, 14 February 1831; apropos of Mozart

Beethoven's talent astonished me; but unhappily his is a quite uncontrolled personality, and while he is indeed far from wrong in finding the world detestable, as a result he makes it no more enjoyable either for himself or for others.
Letter to Karl Friedrich Zelter, 2 September 1812

A name is no trifle. Hasn't Napoleon, for the sake of a great name, broken almost half the world into pieces!
E, 6 April 1829

Napoleon affords an example of the danger of raising oneself to the absolute and sacrificing everything to the execution of an idea. *E*, 10 February 1830

Extraordinary men, like Napoleon, go beyond morality. In the end they act like physical causes, like fire and water.
Riemer, 3 February 1807

It is plain to me that Shakespeare meant to portray a great action laid on a soul unequal to it. Here an oak-tree is planted in a precious vessel which should have received only lovely flowers; the roots expand, the vessel shatters.
WMA; Wilhelm, of Hamlet

It is said that Shakespeare depicted the Romans superbly. I don't see this. They are sheer, inveterate Englishmen, but they are truly human, fundamentally human, and so the Roman toga suits them well enough. Once we have prepared ourselves, we find his anachronisms admirable in the highest degree, for it is exactly his offences against outward forms that make his works so alive. 'Shakespeare Without End', 1815

Shakespeare's finest plays lack facility here and there; they are rather more than they should be, and for that very reason they indicate the great poet.

AA, 1826

Lord Byron is great only as a poet; as soon as he reflects, he is a child.

E, 18 January 1825

Byron's high rank as an English peer was most detrimental to him; for every talent is constrained by the outside world, all the more when there is such high birth and so much money. A middle rank is far more favourable to talent, which is why we find all great artists in the middle classes.

E, 24 February 1825

It still saddens me that Lord Byron, who showed such impatience with the fickle public, wasn't aware of how well the Germans can understand him and how highly they esteem him. With us the moral and political tittle-tattle of the day falls away, leaving the man and the talent standing alone in all their brilliance.

Letter to John Murray, 29 March 1831

We should take care not to be always looking for culture in the determinedly pure and moral. Everything that is great serves to cultivate as soon as we become aware of it.

E, 16 December 1828

The century is ending, but every individual starts from the beginning.

SIP

At all times it is only individuals who have worked for knowledge, not the age. It was the age that put Socrates to death by poison, the age that burnt Huss at the stake: the ages have all been alike.

AA, 1826

The Deed

'In the beginning was the Word', I see.
I'm stuck already! Who can counsel me?
The *Word*? That high I cannot rate it,
Some other way I must translate it ...
The spirit helps! I see how it should read,
And boldly write, 'In the beginning was the *Deed*'.

F1; Faust

I confess that the great and grandiloquent duty, Know Thyself, always seemed suspect to me, as a ruse of priests secretly leagued to confuse men with unachievable demands and seduce them away from active life in the outside world and into a false introspection. Man knows himself only in so far as he knows the world, becoming aware of it only within himself, and of himself only within it. Every new object, closely observed, unlocks a new organ in us.

Natural Science, 1823

How can one get to know oneself? Never by contemplation, but certainly through activity. Try to do your duty, and you will immediately know what is in you. But what is your duty? The demand of the day.

WMT:RMW

If to enter the infinite is your intention,
Simply probe the finite in every direction.

ME

While man still strives, still must he err.

F1, Prologue in Heaven; the Lord

A useless life is an early death.

Iphigenia in Tauris, 1787; Iphigenia

Agreement leaves us at rest, but it is contradiction that makes us productive.

E, 28 March 1827

I see more and more clearly that each of us ought to pursue his own trade seriously and take all the rest lightly. A few verses I have to write interest me more than things of far greater importance in which I have no say. If everyone does the like, things will go well both at home and in the country.

Letter to Karl Ludwig von Knebel, 10 August 1797

Always keep in mind that really we work only for ourselves. If what we do subsequently pleases or serves someone else, then that's good too. But the aim of life is life itself.

Letter to Meyer, 8 February 1796

I don't go in for reminiscence as you do: it's just a clumsy way of expressing oneself. There is nothing in the past we should look back on, there is only an eternal newness, shaping itself out of the diffused elements of the past, and true longing must always be productive, creating what is new and better.

Müller, 4 November 1823

Always hold fast to the present. Every situation, even every moment, is of infinite value, for it is the representative of a whole eternity. *E*, 3 November 1823

Pressure of business is very good for the soul. Once the soul is released, it moves more freely and enjoys life. There is nothing more wretched than a comfortable man without work: the finest of nature's gifts will become nauseous to him.

Diaries, 13 January 1779

Composition is a thoroughly despicable word ... How can one say, Mozart composed *Don Giovanni*! Composition! As if it were a slice of cake or a biscuit stirred together out of eggs, flour and sugar! It is a spiritual creation, in which the parts as well as the whole are of one spirit and outpouring, and pervaded by the breath of one life; so that the producer in no sense tried his hand or patched together or yielded to caprice, but was held in the power of the daemon of his genius, and had to act as this commanded. *E*, 20 June 1831

The surest means of cultivating and preserving a friendship, I find, is for us to communicate turn by turn what we are doing. For people agree far more in what they do than in what they think.

Letter to S.A.W. Herder, December 1798

Work makes companions. *AA*, 1821

The Deed

No productivity of the highest kind, no significant insight, no great fruitful thought, is in anyone's power; these are beyond all earthly authority. We must consider them as unexpected gifts from above, as pure children of God, which we are to receive and revere with joyful thanks. They are related to the daemon, which does with us ineluctably whatever it pleases, and to which we unconsciously submit, while believing we are acting on our own initiative.
E, 11 March 1828

You will find that in middle age a man frequently experiences a turn-about and that, while in his youth everything favoured him, all is now completely changed, and mishaps and disasters are heaped one upon another. But do you know what I think about it? He must be ruined again! Every extraordinary man is called on to perform a certain mission. If he has achieved it, he is no longer needed upon earth in this form, and Providence reuses him for something else.
Ibid.

Thus it was with Napoleon and many others. Mozart died in his thirty-sixth year. Raphael at much the same age. Byron only a little older. But all these had fulfilled their missions to perfection; and it was time for them to go, so that something was still left over for other people to do in a world calculated to last a long while.
Ibid.

Yes, one must be young to do great things ... [reminded of exceptions:] Such men are natural geniuses, theirs is a special case; they experience a renewed puberty, while other people are young only once.
Ibid.

We never go further than when we no longer know where we are going.
SIP

The preoccupation with immortality is for people of rank, and especially women who have nothing to do. But an able man, who intends to pursue a proper trade here, and hence must toil and struggle and labour day by day, leaves the future world to itself and is active and useful in this one.
E, 25 February 1824

I must confess, I wouldn't know how to get along with an eternity of bliss, if it didn't provide me with new tasks and new difficulties to overcome. But that's well catered for; we only have to look at the planets and the suns, plenty of nuts left to crack there.
Müller, 23 September 1827

Authors & Audiences

If the poet daily seizes the present, and always treats what it offers him with freshness of feeling, he will make sure of something good, and if on occasion he doesn't succeed, he loses nothing by it.
E, 18 September 1823

The world is so large and rich, and life so multifarious, that occasions for poems will never be wanting. But they must all be *occasional* poems: that is, reality must give both stimulus and material. A particular case becomes general and poetic by the very fact that it is treated by a poet. All my poems are occasional poems, suggested by real life, and having therein base and bedrock. I think nothing of poems snatched out of the air.
Ibid.

All poetry should be instructive, but imperceptibly; it should guide a man's attention to a sense of what is worth instructing himself in; he must draw the lesson from it himself, as from life.
Letter to Zelter, 29 November 1825

If imagination did not give rise to things that must ever be problematical to the understanding, there would be little for the imagination to do. It is this which separates poetry from prose, where understanding always is and should be at home.
E, 5 July 1827

The poet shouldn't be his own interpreter.
Luden, 19 August 1806

The English poet Thomson wrote a very good poem on the Seasons, but a very bad one on Liberty, and that not from want of poetry in the poet but from want of poetry in the subject. As soon as a poet exerts himself politically, he must give himself up to a party; and once he does that, he is lost as a poet; he must say farewell to his freedom of spirit, his impartial outlook, and pull over his ears the cap of bigotry and blind hatred.
E, early March 1832

Poetry asks, in fact it demands, composure, it isolates man against his will, it repeatedly imposes itself on him, and in the wide world (not to say the great one) is as embarrassing as a faithful mistress.
Letter to Schiller, 9 August 1797

There is something magical about rhythm; it even makes us believe we have taken possession of the sublime.   *AA*, 1824

The rhythm flows unconsciously from the poetic mood. If one thought about it while writing a poem, one would go mad.
E, 6 April 1829

Mysterious and strong effects lie in different poetical forms. If the content of my *Roman Elegies* were transposed into the tone and metre of Byron's *Don Juan*, then what is said would sound quite infamous.   *E*, 25 February 1824

Superstition is the poetry of life; for this reason it doesn't harm the poet to be superstitious.   *AA*, 1823

In poetry there are no contradictions. These exist only in the real world, not in the world of poetry.
Luden, 19 August 1806

There is a poetry without figures of speech which is a single figure of speech.   *AA*, 1823

To be sure, it's the same with poems as with actions; one is in a bad way if they need to be justified.
Letter to Schiller, 29 July 1797

Poets resemble the bear,
Their own paws are their staple fare.

ME

Granted! The poets of the Orient
Are greater than we of the Occident.
But where we are fully their equals
Is in hating our brothers and rivals.
The West-Eastern Divan, 1819

To write prose, one must have something to say; but he who has nothing to say can still make verses and rhymes, where one word suggests the other, and finally something comes out which in fact is nothing but looks as if it were something.
E, 29 January 1827

We poets are much more matter-of-fact people than those who are not poets have any idea of.
Henry Crabb Robinson, 2 August 1829

Why should the poet shrink from picking flowers where he finds them?

> Müller, 17 December 1824; of plagiarism

> A human life, what is it? And yet thousands can
> Talk about the man, and what he did and how he did it.
> A poem is much less; and yet thousands can enjoy it,
> Thousands find fault. My friend, just live, just go on writing!
>
> *VE*

The novel is a subjective epic in which the author requests permission to treat the world in his own way. So the only question is whether he has a way; the rest of it will follow of itself.   *AA*, 1821

I should think a rich manifold life, passing before our eyes, would be enough without any express tendency, which after all is only a concept.

> *E*, 18 January 1825; discussing *Wilhelm Meister's Apprenticeship*

Time and again you will have heard that after people have read a good novel they would like to see it on the stage. But the artist should resist with all his might these childish, tasteless, barbaric tendencies, and keep one work of art separate from another by impenetrable magic circles, preserving the characteristics and peculiarities of each. Yet who can separate his ship from the waves on which it floats? Against storm and wind we make little headway.

> Letter to Schiller, 23 December 1797

The classical is health, the romantic is sickness.   *SIP*

Ovid remained classical even in exile: he looked for his suffering not in himself, but in his separation from the capital of the world.   *Ibid.*

History ought always to consider itself highly honoured when a poet cares to occupy himself with it.

> Soret, 1832

There are three kinds of readers: one, who enjoys without judging; a third, who judges without enjoying; another in the middle, who judges while enjoying and enjoys while judging. The last class truly reproduces a work of art anew; its members are not numerous.

> Letter to Johann Friedrich Rochlitz, 13 June 1819

No one cares to read anything to which he isn't already accustomed in some degree; he demands the familiar, the expected, in a modified form. However, the written word has the advantage that it endures and can wait for the time when it is allowed to take effect.
SIP

The public has a peculiar way of dealing with prominent persons of acknowledged merit; by degrees it grows indifferent to them, and favours talents which, though far inferior, are new; it makes exaggerated demands of the former, and puts up with anything from the latter.

WMA

Nowadays books are not written to be read, and thus to inform and instruct, but to be reviewed, so that people can then talk about them and voice opinions on them and so on *ad infinitum*. Since books began to be reviewed, no one reads them but the reviewer, and he only in snatches. On the other hand, hardly anyone these days has anything to say that's original and illuminating, thought through and worked out by himself with love and diligence; so books get what they deserve.

Riemer, 7 November 1806

It was never perceived by the critics that Werther praised Homer while he retained his senses, and Ossian when he was going mad. But reviewers do not notice such things.

Robinson, 2 August 1829

Criticism makes its appearance like Ate: it pursues authors, but limpingly.
SIP

Authors and the public are separated by an enormous gulf, of which, happily, neither side has any conception. The futility of all prefaces I long ago realised; for the more a writer strives to make his views clear, the more confusion he creates.

PAT, 1814

I was soon acquainted with a related peculiarity of readers, which (particularly in those who print their opinions) strikes me as quite comical. Namely, they labour under the delusion that once he has produced something, a man becomes their debtor; and he always falls far short of what they wanted of him, although before they had come across our work, they hadn't the slightest notion that anything of the kind existed or was even possible.

Ibid.

It was brought home to me, an author of many years' standing, that precisely through presentation copies one can meet apathy and vexation. If someone comes across a book by chance or recommendation, he reads it, he may even buy a copy, but if in easy confidence the author, a friend, presents the opus, it will seem as if he is out to impose his own intellectual predominance thereby.

On Morphology, 'The Fate of the Printed Pamphlet', 1817

Certain books appear to have been written, not in order to teach us anything, but to let us know that the author knew something.

AA, 1821

An old literary truth: What we write pleases us, otherwise we surely wouldn't have written it.

On Morphology, 'The Fate of the Manuscript', 1817

The Arts & Translation

You cannot give the world the slip more certainly than through art, and you cannot bind yourself to it more certainly than through art.
EA:OJ

Its highest purpose must always be to stimulate reflection, and it can only become truly precious to the beholder or reader when it compels him to interpret it in his own way and to complete it, as it were, by re-creation.
Müller, January 1832; of a poem or work of art

Artists are like Sunday's children; they alone see ghosts. But once they have told of these apparitions, everybody sees them.
Karl August Böttiger, December 1797

Apprehension and representation of the particular is the very life of art. And then, while you content yourself with generalities, everybody can imitate you; but in the particular, no one does. Why? Because nobody else has experienced it.
E, 29 October 1823

A good work of art can and will have moral effects, but to demand moral aims of the artist is to ruin his craft.
PAT, 1814

All blossoms must perish, so that the fruits may gladden us;
Blossom and fruit at once only you Muses supply.
Four Seasons, c. 1797

Genuine works of art carry their own aesthetic theory within them, and put into our hands the standards whereby they are to be measured.
Letter to Johann Friedrich Cotta, 14 November 1808

Art is a mediator of the inexpressible, and hence it seems a folly to seek to mediate it afresh through words. Yet endeavouring to do so gains for the understanding a great benefit that in turn improves the practice.
AA, 1827

Beauty can never become clear about itself.

AA, 1824

There is no patriotic art and no patriotic knowledge. Like all that is sublime, both belong to the whole world, and can be promoted only through the mutual and free interaction of all coevals, with constant reference to what remains from the past and is known to us.
WMT:MA

Most people treat a finished work of art as if it were soft clay. According to their inclinations, opinions and whims, the shaped marble is at once to refashion itself, the solidly walled edifice to expand or contract, a painting is to instruct us, a play to improve us, and everything is to be all things.
WMA; the Abbé.

People always talk about studying the ancients; but what does that mean except: turn your attention to the real world, and try to express it? For that is what the ancients did in their day.
E, 29 January 1826

Woe to every kind of culture which destroys the most efficacious means of true culture, and points us to the end instead of making us happy on the way itself!
WMA; Wilhelm

Works of art exist to be seen, not talked about, or at very most in their presence.
IJ, 29 July 1787

A horse with his mane and tail cropped, a hound with clipped ears, a tree whose mightiest branches have been lopped and the rest trimmed into a spherical shape, and above all a young girl whose youthful form has been spoilt and deformed by stays – all these are things from which good taste recoils, and which find a place only in the beauty-catechism of the philistines.
E, 18 April 1827

Technique in alliance with insipidity is the direst enemy of art.
SIP

A hundred times I hear some artist boasting that he owes everything to himself alone! I usually listen to this patiently, but often I retort crossly, 'And it looks like it.'
Letter to Zelter, 23 February 1832

The dignity of art appears most eminently in music, since there is no subject-matter to make allowance for.
WMT:RMW

The Arts & Translation

There is no art in imitating thunder in a piece of music, but the musician who can make me feel as if I were hearing thunder would be very precious. In contrast, utter peace, silence, even negation, have found definite expression in music.

Letter to Adalbert Schöpke, 16 February 1818

Painting is the most indulgent and easy-going of all arts. We let the poorest reproduction pass because we are used to seeing even sorrier original objects.

WMT:RMW

The power of a language doesn't lie in rejecting what is foreign, but in swallowing it up.

SIP

The two ways of translating ancient and modern literature: freely, in accord with the genius and requirements of the people one is translating for, and faithfully, in accord with the genius of the people whose language one is translating from.

Riemer, 13 July 1810

In translating one must on no account get involved in hand-to-hand fighting with the foreign language. One must go all the way to the untranslatable, and respect it; for precisely therein lie the value and the character of every language.

Müller, 20 September 1827

The idioms of every language are untranslatable, for all words, from the highest to the lowest, are related to the peculiar character, fundamental belief and way of life of the people who speak it.

IJ, 5 October 1786

Translators are like busy pimps extolling the surpassing charms of some half-veiled beauty. They excite an irresistible desire for the original.

AA, 1826

Every translator is to be seen as a middleman doing his best in this common spiritual commerce, and making it his business to promote the exchange. For, whatever we may say about the inadequacy of translation, it is and always will be one of the most important and worthiest concerns in the general hustle and bustle of the world. The Koran says, 'God has given every people a prophet in their own tongue.' Hence every translator is a prophet to his people.

Letter to Carlyle, 20 July 1827

Religion

   I know of nothing poorer
   Under the sun than you, you gods!
   Wretchedly you nurture
   Your majesty
   On sacrificial levies
   And the breath of prayers;
   You would go hungry
   Except that children and beggars
   Are hopeful fools.

                                             'Prometheus', 1774

The Christian religion is an intendedly political revolution which, having failed, has turned moral.

                                             SIP

As natural scientists we are pantheists, as poets polytheists, as moral beings monotheists.

                                             Ibid.

   Who has science and art
   Also has religion;
   Who lacks both science and art
   Had better have religion.

                                             ME

Godhead is at work in the living, not in the dead; it is in the becoming and changing, not in the become and the fixed. Thus reason, in its tendency towards the divine, has only to do with the becoming, the living; but understanding with the become, the fixed, that it may make use of it.

                                             E, 13 February 1829

Forgive me for preferring to be silent when the talk is of a divine being. I can see him only in and through *rebus singularibus*. Here I am among hills and under them, seeking the divine in *herbis et lapidibus*.

                                             Letter to Friedrich Heinrich Jacobi, 9 June 1785

Religion

I am a very earthly person; the parables of the Unjust Steward, the Prodigal Son, the Sower, the Pearl of Great Price, the Lost Piece of Silver, etc. etc. are for me more divine (if there is to be something divine) than the Seven Golden Candlesticks, Horns, Seals, Stars and Woes. I too can see the truth, but the truth of the five sense, and may God be patient with me as heretofore.

Letter to Johann Caspar Lavater, Swiss clergyman,
28 October 1779

You hold the Gospels as they stand to be divine truth; but not even an audible voice from heaven would convince me that water burns and fire quenches, that a virgin bears a child, and that a man rises from the dead. Moreover, for me these are blasphemies against God and his revelation in nature. You find nothing more beautiful than the Gospels; I find thousands of records, ancient and modern, written by men inspired by God, just as beautiful, and indispensable to mankind.

Letter to Lavater, 9 August 1782

No doubt all truth comes to us from God; but the Church! There's the point. God speaks to us through this flower and that butterfly; and that's a language these rascals don't understand.

Robinson, 2 August 1829; Goethe 'held a flower in his
hand, and a beautiful butterfly was in the room'

The incurable evil of these religious disputes is that the one party wishes to reduce the highest interest of mankind to fairy tales and empty words, and the other proposes to base it on what satisfies no one.

SIP

> Jews and heathens out! Thus the fervent Christian's tolerance.
> Accursed be Christians and heathens! mutters a bearded Jew.
> Christians be skewered and Jews burnt on the bonfire!
> Chants a young Turk, mocking both the one and the other.
> Which is the wisest? You judge! But if any of these fools
> Dwell in your palace, Divinity, then I shall pass by.

VE

Whoever feels his heart in need
Finds a prophet no matter where.

Satyros, 1773

As a man is, so is his God born;
That's why God is so often held to scorn.

ME

When I see a pilgrim, I can never hold my tears back.
  How a mistaken idea can make us humans happy!

VE

What use to you, poor girl, is a part of the crucified god?
  Call for Priapus' part, so much more salubrious.

Ibid.; on religious relics

'Why are you so cruel, wanting to rob Christians of the
    blessings
  Of faith?' Not I; no one could possibly do such a thing,
For it's down in black and white: The heathen rage in vain.
    And so
  I fulfil the scriptures: read and be uplifted by me.

VE

You know how much I respect Christianity; or perhaps you don't. These days who is a Christian in the way Christ would have us be? I alone, perhaps, though you all consider me a heathen.

Müller, 7 April 1830

I a heathen? After all, I had Gretchen executed and Ottilie starve to death. Isn't that Christian enough for these people? What do they want that's more Christian?

Karl August Varnhagen von Ense, December 1809

Little by little we shall all move increasingly from a Christianity of words and faith to a Christianity of feeling and action. *E*, 11 March 1832

Let us remain untroubled about the future! In our Father's kingdom are many provinces; as he has prepared such a happy settlement for us on earth, so shall we both be surely provided for above.

Letter to Countess Auguste Bernstorff, née Stolberg,
17 April 1823; she had urged Goethe to 'turn his
eyes and heart from earth to heaven'

Let those who believe in immortality enjoy their happiness in silence; they have no reason to put on airs.

E, 25 February 1824

Man should believe in immortality; he has a right to believe in it; it accords with his nature, and he may build on the promises of religion. But if the philosopher tries to deduce the immortality of the soul from a legend, this is feeble and amounts to very little. My faith in our continuance derives from the idea of activity; for if I work on unflaggingly till my death, nature is bound to allot me another form of existence when the present one can no longer sustain my spirit.

E, 16 December 1828

Nature & Science

Nature has neither kernel
Nor shell,
Nature is all things together.
Put yourself to the test – whether
You are kernel or shell.

'To be sure', 1820

Nature's spectacle is always new, because she creates new spectators. Life is her most abundant invention, and death is her trick for securing abundant life.

'Nature', *Tiefurt Journal*, 1782-3; an essay by G.C. Tobler,
a young Swiss, based on conversations with Goethe
and, the latter said, reflecting his thinking at the time

Man obeys her laws, even when he opposes them; man works with her, even when he means to work against her.

Ibid.

You are confused, beloved, by the thousandfold mixture
   Of these teeming flowers that envelop the garden ...
All their forms are alike, yet none the same as another,
   And in this way the chorus points to a secret law,
A sacred riddle ...

'The Metamorphosis of Plants', 1798

Nature doesn't worry herself over some error; she herself can only and ever act correctly, without worrying, whatever may follow from it.

SIP

That nature does nothing in vain is an old philistine saying. She works ever vitally, superfluously and prodigally, so that the infinite may be constantly present, for nothing can last.

Letter to Zelter, 13 August 1831

Nature is an organ which the Lord God plays on while the Devil blows the bellows.

Johann Sulpiz Boisserée, 8 September 1815

The true, identical with the divine, never lets us perceive it directly. We see it only as reflection, example, symbol, in individual and related manifestations; we become aware of it as incomprehensible, and yet we cannot renounce the wish to comprehend it.
On Meteorology, 1825

We only really know anything when we know little; as knowledge grows, so does doubt.
AA, 1826

Man must persist in the faith that the incomprehensible is comprehensible; otherwise he would abandon his investigations.
WMT:RMW

The highest happiness of man as a thinking being is to have fathomed what is fathomable and quietly to revere what is unfathomable.
SIP

When nature begins to reveal her manifest mystery, we feel an irresistible longing for her worthiest interpreter – art.
AA, 1823

It strikes me as very remarkable that science, which in its origins was shrouded in mystery, must again, in its unending development, turn into a mystery.
Letter to Seebeck, 29 April 1812

Man is indeed a strange creature! When I got to know how a kaleidoscope works, I lost interest in it. Dear God could throw us into considerable embarrassment by revealing all the secrets of nature; we wouldn't know what to be doing for apathy and boredom.
Riemer, June 1818

Theories are generally the overhastiness of an impatient mind which wants to get rid of phenomena and therefore replaces them with pictures, concepts, often even mere words.
Natural Science, 1823

Nature doesn't give herself to each and everyone. Towards many she behaves more like a saucy young girl, who entices us with a thousand charms, but in the moment when we think we have grasped and possessed her, slips out of our arms.
Soret, 2 August 1831

If, on investigating natural objects, I formed an opinion, I didn't expect nature to assent at once; but rather, I pursued her with observations and experiments, and was satisfied if she proved obliging enough to confirm my opinion on occasion. If she didn't, at any rate she brought me to some other insight, which I followed through and which perhaps I found her more willing to endorse.

E, 1 October 1828

I have noticed that the best discoverers are not those who possess the deepest knowledge. The child with his nose close to the ground is often the first to see the insect crawling on the surface because he isn't thinking of the possibility of a meteor, which would tempt him to watch the sky and lose sight of his modest research.

Soret, 25 May 1824

As if things exist only when they can be mathematically demonstrated! It would be foolish for a man not to believe in his mistress's love because she couldn't prove it to him mathematically. She can prove her dowry mathematically, but not her love.

E, 20 December 1826; mathematics 'a noble science' but not to be applied to matters outside its sphere

The finest metempsychosis is when we see ourselves appearing again in others.

On Morphology, 1822

Of what use is the expenditure of suns and planets and moons, of stars and galaxies, of comets and nebulae, of evolved and evolving worlds, unless at last a happy man rejoices unconsciously in his existence?

Winckelmann and his Century, 1805

War & Revolution

War is in truth a disease in which the juices of the body that make for health and preservation are used to nourish an intruder at odds with the constitution.

Riemer, 13 December 1806

Our modern wars make many miserable while they last and nobody happy when they are over.

IJ, 6 September 1787

> War and trade and piracy,
> An indivisible trinity.

F2; Mephistopheles

A battle is a battle, and the situations it offers are well-worn. And what has the German victory to do with me, that I too should give ear to the shouts of triumph? Why, I can shout myself. Make me feel something I haven't felt, think something I haven't thought, and I will praise you. But noise and shouting instead of pathos, that won't do. Tinsel and nothing more.

Letter to Friederike Oeser, 13 February 1769

For me, since I am not of a warlike nature and have no warlike sense, war-songs would have been a mask fitting my face very ill. I have never affected anything in my poetry. I have never uttered anything I have not experienced. I have made love-songs only when I have loved. How could I write songs of hatred without hating!

E, 14 March 1830

> The great went to the wall; but who protected the masses
>   Against the masses? The masses were tyrants to the masses.

VE; of the French Revolution

Before the revolution it was all striving; afterwards all is changed into demanding.

SIP

I was perfectly convinced that any great revolution is never a fault of the people, but always of the government. Revolutions are utterly impossible as long as governments are constantly just and constantly alert. Because I hated revolutions I have been named a 'friend of the status quo'. But that's a very ambiguous title, which I beg to decline. If the existent were wholly excellent, good and just, I would certainly have nothing against it, but since, together with much that is good there is also much that is bad, unjust, imperfect, a friend of the status quo often means little less than a friend of the obsolete and bad.

E, 4 January 1824

Once and for all I'm supposed to be no friend to the people. I am indeed no friend to the revolutionary rabble, whose object is robbery, arson, and murder, and who, behind the mask of the public weal, have their eyes only on the meanest egotistical aims. I am no friend to such people, any more than I am a friend of a Louis XV. I hate every violent overthrow, because as much good is destroyed thereby as is gained. I hate those who carry it out, as well as those who give cause for it. But am I therefore no friend to the people?

E, 27 April 1825

Had I the misfortune to find myself in the opposition, I would rather stir up turmoil and revolution than hang around in those murky circles forever finding fault with the existing state of affairs.

Müller, 3 February 1823

Freedom, Law & Order

Only in limitation is mastery shown
And law alone can give us freedom.

'Nature and Art', 1802

You have only to declare yourself free, and straight away you will feel yourself constrained. But be bold enough to declare yourself constrained, and you will feel yourself free.

EA:OJ

It is not by refusing to acknowledge anything superior to us that we are made free, but precisely by revering what is superior. For, in revering it, we raise ourselves to it.

E, 18 January 1827

Whenever I hear talk of liberal ideas, I marvel how men like to amuse themselves with empty sounds. An idea can't be liberal! Let it be vigorous, efficient, self-contained, so that it may fulfil its divine mission of being creative. Still less can a concept be liberal, for it has a totally different function. But where we must look for liberality is in the sentiments, and these are the living spirit. Yet sentiments are rarely liberal, because sentiment stems directly from personality and its immediate relations and needs.

AA, 1823

True liberalism is acknowledgement.

SIP

Which government is the best? The one that teaches us to govern ourselves.

AA, 1826

To rule is easy to learn, to govern is hard.

SIP

Lawgivers or revolutionaries who promise equality and liberty at the same time are dreamers or charlatans.

Ibid.

> Those apostles of freedom, they always disgusted me,
>   In the end each of them sought absolute power for
>   himself.
> If you want to free many, then dare to serve many.
>   You want to know how dangerous that is? Just try it.
>
>   *VE*

I am always for a firm adherence to a law, particularly at a time like the present, when too much is everywhere being lightly conceded out of weakness and exaggerated liberalism.

E, 19 February 1831; of the law concerning inoculation against smallpox

It is better that injustices occur than that they are redressed by unjust means.

SIP

I would rather commit an injustice than tolerate disorder.
The Siege of Mainz, 1793; on failing to punish a guilty party

Only those cry out for the freedom of the press who want to abuse it.

SIP

The [French] law curbing the press can only prove beneficial, especially as its restraints concern nothing fundamental, but merely apply to personalities. An opposition that knows no bounds is a flat affair; restraints perforce sharpen its wits, which is most advantageous. To voice an opinion directly and coarsely is excusable only when one is wholly right. A party, precisely because it is a party, cannot be wholly in the right, and hence the indirect method, in which the French have always been models, serves well.

E, 9 July 1827

The underdog, since he cannot act, may at least express himself in speech. 'Let them sing,' said Mazarin when he was shown satirical songs on a new tax, 'just as long as they pay!'

SIP

Order of any kind turns eventually into pedantry; to get rid of the latter, men destroy the former, and so it goes for a time, until men see they must again create order.

AA, 1826

If a man studied all the laws, he would have no time to break any.

AA, 1823

Laws are all made by the old and by men. Women and the young want the exceptions, the old the rules.

WMT:MA

We respect an old foundation, but we mustn't waive the right to base ourselves somewhere else.

WMT:RMW; on authority

If you demand duties of people without granting them rights, you must pay them well.

AA, 1823

Practically all laws are syntheses of the impossible; for example, the institution of marriage. And yet it is good that this is so, for through postulating the impossible we strive towards the maximum possible.

Müller, 19 October 1823

Truths & Errors

It is as certain as it is strange that truth and error come from the same source; which is why we are often deterred from attacking error since at the same time we harm truth.

AA, 1821

The worst of it is that thinking doesn't help us towards thought; we must be right by nature, so that good ideas may constantly come to us like free children of God, and cry, 'Here we are.'

E, 24 February 1824

Thinking is more interesting than knowing; but not than observing.

SIP

One always thinks of oneself as seeing. I believe we have dreams simply so that we don't stop seeing.

EA:OJ

There is a lot we would know better if we didn't wish to define it too precisely.

WMT:RMW

We do not do well to spend too long among abstractions. The esoteric is harmful only when it attempts to become exoteric. Life is best instructed by what is living.

WMT:MA

General ideas and great conceit are always on the way to causing dreadful misfortune.

WMT:RMW

> What is the general?
> The single case.
> What is the special?
> Millions of cases.

Ibid.

Writing history is a way of shaking off the past.

AA, 1821

If wise men didn't err, fools would be in despair.

SIP

Many are proud of what they know; and towards what they don't know, haughty.

Ibid.

It makes no difference whether someone speaks true or false; either way he will be contradicted.

Ibid.

Opponents think they are refuting us when they repeat their own opinions and pay no attention to ours.

Ibid.

Unfortunately it is the same with dietetic matters as with moral: we cannot see into a mistake until we are rid of it. In which case nothing is gained since the next mistake doesn't resemble the one before and hence cannot be recognised under the same form.

PAT, 1812

If we haven't seen the newspapers for some months and then read them all together, we come to realise how much time is thrown away on these rags.

SIP

Then nowadays there is the ease with which every error can at once be universally promulgated by means of the press.

E, 13 February 1831

When I see a misprint I always think something new has been invented.

SIP

Unfortunately, for men words are commonly surrogates; for the most part they think and know better than they articulate.

WMT:MA

Snow is a false cleanliness.

AA, 1821

The smallest hair casts a shadow.

Ibid.

A rainbow which lasts for a quarter of an hour is looked at no longer.

Ibid.

A hundred grey horses don't make a single white horse.

SIP

> Wanted: a small dog
> That neither bites nor snarls,
> Feeds on broken glass
> And shits pearls.

'Advertisement', *ME*

The Hindus of the desert take a solemn vow to eat no fish.

AA, 1821

The tiger, who wants to make the deer understand how delightful it is to slurp blood.

SIP

Do those who are fortunate believe that he who is unfortunate should die in front of them decently, as the Roman mob used to expect of a gladiator?

AA, 1824

When someone is grieving over his lost income, his ruined career, it would be inhuman not to sympathise; but if he believes that as a consequence the whole world is even in the slightest degree going to the dogs, I am quite unable to agree.

Letter to Zelter, 27 July 1807

We look back on our life only as a thing of broken fragments, because our omissions and failures are always the first to strike us and outweigh in imagination our deeds and successes.

On Morphology, 1822

Death is, so to speak, an impossibility which suddenly becomes a reality.

Soret, 15 February 1830

What a poor show is made by those necrologists who, immediately after a man has gone, sedulously juxtapose the good and the bad, balancing his so-called virtues against his so-called weaknesses with hypocritical righteousness, and in this way, far worse than death, destroy a personality which can be conceived only in the living union of such opposed qualities.

Letter to Zelter, 29 May 1801

Various sayings of the ancients, which we are wont to repeat again and again, had a quite different meaning from the one we tend to give them in later times.

WMT:MA

The Man Himself

My soul is changed a little. I am no more a thunderer as I was at Francfort. Many time I become a melancholical one. I know not whence it comes. Then I look on every man with a starring owl like countenance. In like situation of my soul, I make english verses, english verses, that a stone would weep. In that moment thou shallt have of them. Think on it sister thou art a happy maiden, to have a brother who makes english verses. I pray thee be not haugty thereof.

> Letter from Leipzig, written in English, 11 May 1766, when Goethe was 16, to his sister, Cornelia, a year younger

Often Sister I am in good humor. In a very good humor! Then I go to visit pretty wifes and pretty maiden. St! Say nothing of it to the father. – But why should the father not know it. It is a very good scool for a young fellow to be in the company and acquaintance of young virtuos and honest ladies. The fear to be hatred by them makes us fly many excesses seducing by his outward side, and therefore periculous to the Youth.

> As above, 14 May 1766

From Werther's Sorrows
Still more from his Joys
Good Lord, deliver us!

> 'Hasty Prayer', c. 1775; the critic Friedrich Nicolai had written a parody of *The Sorrows of Young Werther* called *The Joys of Young Werther*, 1775

I have lived through wild times, and have not failed
   To be foolish myself, as the time commanded me.   *VE*

The holy ones, so it's said, wished sinners of both sexes
   Especially well. But it's just the same with me.   *Ibid.*

Do you know, you epigrams, how I can make you
   By the hundred? Just remove me from my beloved!
                                                Ibid.

Had I been born an Englishman, I would have been a rich duke, or rather a bishop with an annual income of 30,000 pounds sterling.   Soret, 17 March 1830

> Had God wanted me different,
> He would have built me differently.
>
> *Tame Xenia*, 1820-7

For me it was the same with these inquiries into natural phenomena as with my poems; I did not make them, but they made me.

Campaign in France, entry dated 30 August 1792

To make use of experience has always been everything with me; it was never my custom to invent out of thin air, I have always considered the world a greater genius than myself.

Anon. memoirist, 1809, probably F.A. Wolf

This Goethe was so complete a realist that he simply wasn't to be persuaded that objects as such exist only in so far as they are perceived by the cognitive subject. 'What!' he once said, with his Jove-like eyes fixed on me, 'Light exists only in so far as you see it? No! You wouldn't exist if the light didn't see you.'

Arthur Schopenhauer, n.d.

I shall never rest until I know that my ideas are derived, not from words or tradition, but from contact with the living things themselves.

IJ, 27 June 1787

But nothing done as a trade! That is repugnant to me. Everything I can do I want to do as a game, whatever it is and for as long as it gives me pleasure ... Useful? The usefulness is your affair. You can use me; but I cannot prepare myself for sale or demand ... I won't be turned into an instrument; and every trade is an instrument.

Riemer, January 1807

It is strange, that with all the various things I have done, there is not one of my poems that could appear in the Lutheran hymn-book.

E, 4 January 1827

It is dreary to listen to political talk, from whatever quarter. To free myself from the like, as also from aesthetic conversations and lectures, for six weeks I have given myself to the service of a very pretty child, and thus was perfectly protected from all external rigours.

Letter to Zelter, 24 August 1823; the pretty child was Ulrike von Levetzow

People were never basically satisfied with me, and always wished me otherwise than it had pleased God to make me ... In religious, scientific and political matters, it constantly caused trouble for me that I was no hypocrite and had the courage to speak my mind. I believed in God and in Nature and in the triumph of good over evil; but this wasn't enough for pious souls: I was also to believe that three is one and one is three, which ran counter to my innermost feeling for truth. Besides, I didn't see that such beliefs would be of the slightest use to me.

E, 4 January 1824

I am indeed no anti-Christian, no un-Christian, but decidedly a non-Christian.

Letter to Lavater, 29 July 1782

More and more I find it necessary to be on the side of the minority, which is always more intelligent.

Müller, 6 March 1828

I am glad there is something I hate; for otherwise one is in danger of falling into the dull habit of literally finding all things good in their place – and that is destructive of all true feeling.

Robinson, April 1804

When I first began to write, I made it a principle never to dedicate anything to anyone, so that I should never come to repent it.

Said to Napoleon at a meeting recorded by
Prince Talleyrand, 2 October 1808

If a stranger now comes with spectacles, I immediately think, 'He hasn't read my latest poems!' and that in itself is a little to his disadvantage; or 'He has read them, he knows their peculiarity, and sets them at naught', and that's still worse.

E, 5 April 1830

Tell me, where did you learn that bad habit?

J.W.K. Zahn, 7 September 1827; during a dinner
given by Goethe, Zahn added water to his wine

People are always talking about originality, but what does it mean? As soon as we are born the world begins to work upon us, and this goes on till the end. And anyway, what can we call our own apart from energy, strength and will! If I could declare everything I have owed to great predecessors and contemporaries, there wouldn't be much left over.

E, 12 May 1825

> I'd like to break free from tradition,
> And be an original – surely
> The highest honour I would reckon,
> Were it not that, very strangely,
> I am myself a tradition.
>
> *ME*

I don't know myself, and God forbid that I should.

E, 10 April 1829

They come and ask: what idea did I seek to incorporate in my *Faust*? – As if I knew it myself and could express it!

E, 6 May 1827

> 'How did you get so far, then?
> So much, they say, you have wrought!'
> My child, simply through acumen –
> I have never thought about thought.
>
> *ME*

I would rather an injurious truth than a useful error,
   For truth assuages the pain it can cause in us.

Four Seasons, c. 1797

Having from the first been convinced, and still more so of late years, that newspapers exist essentially to string the multitude along and delude it for a time – whether because some external force prevents the editor from telling the truth, or because internal party feeling similarly forbids him – I have given up reading them.

Annals, 1808

What! Have I reached the age of eighty just to go on thinking the same thing? On the contrary, I strive each day to think something different, something new, to avoid turning into a bore. One must constantly change, renew, and rejuvenate oneself, if one isn't to grow fusty.

Müller, 24 April 1830; on being told that his opinions
on various matters used to be quite different

For the present my chief doctrine is this: that the father should look after his house, the tradesman his trade, the priest mutual love, and that the police shouldn't be spoilsports.

Soret, 20 October 1830

I am not born to be a tragic poet, for I am conciliatory by nature. So a case of pure tragedy cannot interest me, since for this there must truly be no reconciliation, and it seems quite absurd to me that there could be anything unreconcilable in this otherwise flat world.

Letter to Zelter, 31 October 1831

I find myself as little in harmony with the artist as with his picture ... These things are nothing but negations of life. To begin with, the death of nature, the winter landscape: I do not acknowledge winter; then monks, fugitives from life, buried alive: I do not acknowledge monks; then a monastery, a ruined one to be sure, but I do not acknowledge monasteries; and finally, to cap it all, even a dead man, a corpse: but I do not acknowledge death.

Förster, 1826; concerning a painting of a procession
of monks in the snow, following the coffin of one of
their brothers to his grave in a ruined monastery

All things the gods give, the infinite,
To their darlings totally,
All joys, the infinite,
All pains, the infinite, totally.

1777; on the death of his sister, Cornelia

The whole profit of my life
Is to lament her loss.

6 June 1816; on the death of his wife, Christiane

Like a star, without haste, but without rest.

Tame Xenia, 1820-7; impression on a seal presented
to Goethe on his 82nd birthday by Carlyle
and other English admirers

He died the most blessed of deaths, conscious and cheerful, with no premonition of dying right until his last breath, and with no pain at all. The vital flame gradually and gently sank and went out without a struggle. His last request was for light; half an hour before the end he told them: 'Open the shutters, to let more light in.'

Müller, 22 March 1832, the day of Goethe's death